Why We Write Poetry

"Poetry is a way to distort the usual mirror we hold up to reality, to play with shards and angles and capture something that conjures fresh feelings, memories, insights—something perhaps less accurate, but truer."
— Jeff Book

"Poetry chooses each of us; the only question is how we choose to express it. Poetry connects me to this world through a song of honesty, joy, pain and appreciation that resonates and reverberates—because I need to sing it as much as I hope there are ears open to hearing it."
— Mel Campbell

"I write poems because they are not as long as novels or even short stories, but even so, allow the writer to share his perceptions of life."
— Jim Ferguson

"Sometimes, I have something to say, and poetry is a way for me to say it."
— Tom Gordon

"My writing of poetry through the years has been like a spiritual journal, tracking my thoughts and responses to loves, losses, friendships, politics, and life events."
— Charles Kinnaird

"Only metaphor gave Noah a place to land."
— Shannon Webster

"To release the power of imagery and idea from words."
— Steve Coleman

"I write poetry to reconnect to myself, to decipher and unravel the conflicting voices in my head, to broaden and grow my self-awareness and my appreciation of life, to engage and love my family and friends, to nurture a poetry family and community, and to develop my spiritual vision. Full seeing seems to take most of our lifetime."
— Roger Carlisle

"I love the discipline of pushing words around in an effort to line them up to make lovely sounds and to express a thought in a succinct manner."
— Chervis Isom

"I'm not much for dancing, and it's too windy to throw rocks."
— statement unclaimed by anyone

Poems *for* Hungry Minds

2022

Poems *for* Hungry Minds

2022

A Publication of HIGHLAND AVENUE POETS

Birmingham, Alabama

Copyright © 2022 by Highland Avenue Poets Publishing

All rights to individual poems reside with the artist himself, and he affirms that his work is his original creation. No part of this book may be reproduced, stored in a retrieval system, or transmitted in any form without written permission from the artist himself.

Any representation of persons is entirely fictional. The views expressed within the poems in this anthology do not necessarily reflect the views of other poets of the anthology.

Steve Coleman, Managing Editor

Address all inquiries to:
highlandavepoets@gmail.com.

Photos and Illustrations from Tom Gordon

Cover and interior design by The Book Cover Whisperer: OpenBookDesign.biz

979-8-9869814-1-3 Paperback
979-8-9869814-0-6 Hardcover
979-8-9869814-2-0 eBook

FIRST EDITION

TO
BARRY MARKS

*Our founder, mentor, critic and encourager, whose
zeal for poetry has taught us all so much.*

AN ACCOMPLISHED ATTORNEY AND poet, Barry is the author of several books of poetry and has been a teacher and leader of poetry in Alabama for 25 years. His poetry collections include: *My Father Should Die in Winter* (2021, Brick Road Poetry Press); *Dividing by Zero* (2015, Negative Capability Press); *Sounding* (2012, Negative Capability Press) (finalist for the Eric Hoffer Award for Independent Publishers); and *Possible Crocodiles* (2010, Brick Road Poetry Press) (named 2010 Book of the Year by the Alabama State Poetry Society). Barry's interest in spanning creative forms is demonstrated by a poetry/music collaboration, *Sometimes Y*, with Professor Alan Goldspiel, University of Montevallo, which has been performed at music conferences and universities around the country. Barry was Alabama's Poet of the Year for 1999 and twice President of the Alabama State Poetry Society.

Contents

Preface i

THE CRAFT 1

   Sitting in Minerva's Kitchen
      Charles Kinnaird 3

   Desirée
      Steve Coleman 5

A TASTE OF NATURE 7

   Ode to a(n) (O)Possum
      Jim Ferguson 9

   In the Yucatan
      Jeff Book 11

   Snow Day
      Roger Carlisle 13

   Life
      Steve Coleman 15

   Trees Soothe My Soul
      Roger Carlisle 17

   Underground, Unknowing
      Tom Gordon 19

   Emerald Coast
      Jim Ferguson 21

   The Lost Comfort of Gardens (March 2022)
      Tom Gordon 23

RECONNECTIONS 27

   Privateers
      Shannon Webster 29

On His First Day of Second Grade
Mel Campbell 31

The Time Between Us
Charles Kinnaird 33

Defiance
Tom Gordon 35

Been Painting My Boat
Steve Coleman 37

Morning Light
Charles Kinnaird 39

Nice Ride
Jeff Book 41

A Life at the Pool
Roger Carlisle 43

Once and Then
Steve Coleman 45

SIGHTS, SMELLS, SOUNDS 47

Stone Pathways
Charles Kinnaird 49

Photograph Birmingham Bus Stop – 7 A.M.
Chervis Isom 51

Piled Higher and Deeper
Jim Ferguson 53

For Naught
Tom Gordon 55

Philosophy 101
Shannon Webster 57

Cleaving
Steve Coleman 59

TIMES OF WAR 61

Resignation (March 2022)
Tom Gordon. 63

The Blood of Patriots
Jeff Book. 65

You, Vladimir
Tom Gordon. 67

What Can We Do?
Steve Coleman 69

Bricks in Kyivian Gates
Mel Campbell. 71

After the War
Charles Kinnaird 73

This Is Not Ukraine
Tom Gordon. 75

Appomattox
Charles Kinnaird 77

GOOD LOVE/BAD LOVE. 79

The Day Before Easter: A Prose Poem
Chervis Isom 81

Rembrandt's Prodigal Son (Hermitage Museum, St. Petersburg, Russia)
Roger Carlisle. 85

Steel City Eurydice
Mel Campbell. 87

Omelets and Petals
Tom Gordon. 89

Northwest Passage
Jim Ferguson 91

A Cruel Rain
Shannon Webster 93

Slip Knot
Jeff Book..................................... 95

The Anomaly: A Sonnet
Chervis Isom 97

FINAL COURSE 99

For Bill Buckner
Mel Campbell................................ 101

Scene from My Father's Wake
Charles Kinnaird 103

Those Emerald Green Eyes: A Villanelle
Chervis Isom 105

A Family Listens to Their Mother
Roger Carlisle............................... 107

Next
Steve Coleman 109

Extremities
Jeff Book.................................... 111

Letting Go
Shannon Webster 113

The Human Spirit
Chervis Isom 115

Frozen Ground
Roger Carlisle............................... 117

Palm Sunday
Jim Ferguson 119

The End
Jim Ferguson 121

WHAT REMAINS 123
Watching from a Distance
Mel Campbell............................... 125
InCredo
Shannon Webster 127
Oblation
Shannon Webster 129

Contributor Biographies 131

Preface

THIS ANTHOLOGY GATHERS THE voices, wisdom, community, fellowship, and longing for a better world through awareness, deep examination, and the joy of poetry. The HIGHLAND AVENUE POETS* are a long-standing community of southern poets meeting monthly to workshop, edit and collectively refine their work.

Poetry slows the urgent world and grants a focus on life within it. The discipline practiced by these authors has occasioned a kind of communal joy - poems that reflect a community of compassion for the world.

You are invited within.

---

*In June 2020, Highland Avenue Poets under the group's original name, Highland Avenue Eaters of Words, published *The Social Distance: Poetry in Response to Covid-19*.

The Craft

Sitting in Minerva's Kitchen

I first met poetry as a warm starry night – and
cloudless.
Speechless joy, dazzling and calm.
Steadfast. Ever-moving.
No desire to leave.
She was a quieting immensity.
I later discovered
I had only seen one fin of the whale,
heard one note of the symphony
– thought it profound.
When I found her more beautiful
than a thousand artists' portrayals,
I needed to recover from the sight.

Rilke warned,
"Beauty is nothing but the beginning of terror."
When the ground gave way
causing my heart to race,
I sought a moment to breathe the calming
    rhythm
of a starry night;
a chance to clothe myself
in ordinary time.

A poet's muse holds magnificent joy
and holy terror –

one welcomes
the distraction of a vanilla friend,
a wordless cup of tea.
There is respite
in that long deep breath
while sitting
in Minerva's kitchen
during ordinary time;
thankful for memories
of holy terror,
thankful for a wooden chair
and a cup of tea.

~ CHARLES KINNAIRD

Desirée

I have a cat
named Desirée
Not treats but birds
she craves

Gazing window's vista
she spots a hawk
Red-tail raptor's best
delicious catch

Furious scratches
on clear hard glass
Hawk soars by
Empty sky

Aspiring cat
oh Desirée
Reflect my own
humbled attempts to write

I share your wish
a fervent dream
to snare
a bird in flight.

~ Steve Coleman

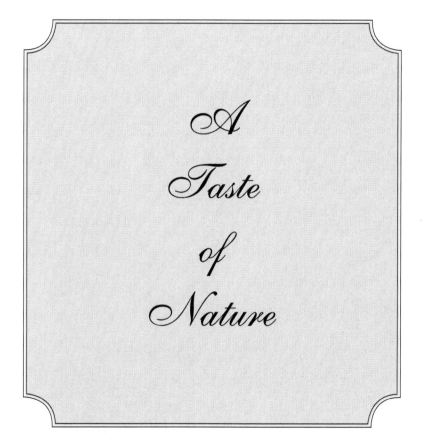

ODE TO A(N) (O)POSSUM

O, opossum, your first letter
O is as silent as you
Operating through the night
On platypus feet
On darkened roads
Opting for the indigestible
Offal parasitic and insect chow
Oh my!

Or might your first O be official
Ostentatious, merely ornamental
Open like your mouth consuming
Over and over and over
Oceanic volumes of microbes
Organisms of odious consistency
Off-putting to others
Oui?

Or not; you offer originality
Olfactory receptors perfected
Oscillating whiskers sensing
Opportunities to cleanse
Old earth of ominous omicron—
Omnivorous yes, yet Orpheus,
Orca, and orchids, laud you
O, Opossum!

~ JIM FERGUSON

In the Yucatan

Trilling and honking,
A flamboyance of flamingos
Clouds the lagoon, strutting
And preening, hobnobbing
Like guests at a cocktail party
(Some as still as swizzle sticks),
Like leggy showgirls and as
Bedazzling, radiant in pink, all
Rosy charisma. How amazing
That flamingos fledge gray,
Like clay pots before glazing,
Or the manmade mountains
That rise from this jungle, the
Timeworn temples of the Maya.
Once they too were riots of color,
Their lavish hues as vibrant
In the fierce sun as the
Still-beating heart freed from
A captive warrior's chest—hot
Blood to slake their shrines.
That they did this, my guide explains,
Meant not that life was cheap but
Dear, a worthy gift for the gods.
I imagine the high priest scaling
The gaudy pyramid, clad in the
Skin of the heartless warrior,
Headdress resplendent with

Beads and bright feathers.
The temples met their
Monochrome fate.
The flamingos shine on—till
Daylight bleeds from the sky
And all fades to gray.

~ Jeff Book

Snow Day

Roads closed, a vacation day,
excitement locked inside
by white drifts of snow.

Millions of snowflakes falling,
snow on snow all day long,
the landscape's invitation to forget.

Wrapped in a blanket of peace,
I fear the limits of time will
disappear in the silence.

It feels like evening all day,
a frozen stillness, a quiet day of rest.
Only the cardinals know how to celebrate.

~ Roger Carlisle

LIFE

A pinecone fell
cone seeds spawned
Then four thousand years
of volcano violence,
vicious winds

Bristlecone Pine
sun seared
lightning scorched
no rain for days

beasts struggled
wars waged
plagues raged
double helix DNA

The tree grown tall
"Methuselah" yet survives
Eternal life is on my mind.

~ Steve Coleman

Found on a western slope in California, the oldest living Bristlecone Pine, "Methuselah" is over 4,850 years old.

Trees Soothe My Soul

When I opened the door,
I found the trees whispering
in a harmonious rhythm,
branches bowing to one another,
pheromones signaling danger,
roots stretching, crackling underground.

My abrupt entrance hushed their emerald breaths,
the way a homeless man disrupts a church service,
everyone acting as if they're in a superior tribe,
as if the sermon had ended before he arrived.

I love the glimpse I had of these
caring spirits, exposing the
peace in their community of wisdom,
energy in their shared silence.

Next time I'll be a cautious sunbeam,
open the door by inches,
stand silently in awe.

~ Roger Carlisle

Underground, Unknowing

You do not live in a world of names.
You cannot know and cannot care
that another species that calls itself human
calls you a Blind Mole Rat,
says you are related to mice,
that you are vegetarian,
have sex with multiple partners,
grow up to a foot in length,
live in tunnels you dig
with two sharp front teeth,
have tiny eyes that barely see
but can sense when
a light shaft breaches your world
and when a hole must be plugged.
You do not count anything.
Humans do.
They say your numbers
are fifteen thousand, maybe more,
and some of you live in a land
they call Ukraine.

Foxes and owls like to eat you.
That's why you live in tunnels.
You will fight when cornered
but in Ukraine,
owls and foxes do not threaten you now,
just things the humans call shells
that shake the ground above you,
cause tunnel walls to fall and bury
your latest mate and her babies,
make a whine your sharp ears
have never before heard
and rip open your world
to a light you cannot plug,
claw, or bite.

Your forebears endured this.
Now it's your turn to be
in something the humans
call war. The human who started it
knows nothing about you,
and his fellow creatures now hiding
in Ukrainian tunnels
consider him a life form
not worthy of the name
you unknowingly bear.

~ Tom Gordon

Emerald Coast

Becalmed the tide at noon
Low spectacle now this layered sea
With waves like frosting thinly spread
When ladled gently from a spoon.
How differently it crashed last night!
White-capped and roaring ancient maw
Spiked and jagged and rusty-tined
Summoned by the darkened moon

While we slept. Today children leave
Their pails in sparkling pools
Where small fish glimmer and gleam
Seaweed blades a green garland weave
And we, beached dozing and deserted fools—
Seek harbor in a dream; seek harbor in a dream.

~ Jim Ferguson

The Lost Comfort of Gardens
(March 2022)

On a fall afternoon, so quiet
a bird call flew static free
across the valley,
so still you could hear
an oncoming car
long before you saw it,
I saw a French couple
kneeling side by side in a garden
they must have maintained for years.

From where I stood,
I could not tell
exactly what they were doing,
but whether
it was planting, picking, or weeding,
it was clear they were nurturing
a patch of earth that brought
nourishment and beauty
to their wizened stone home,
and maybe more than enough bounty
to sell at a church square on market day.

Perhaps, 20 years later,
the man and woman are still there,
still kneeling, digging, pulling, planting,
tiring more easily,
spades and hoes rusted,

rubber boots mud-pimpled,
trousers mud-frayed,
all reassuringly redolent of sweat
and the life-giving dirt of the earth.

I have never touched
Ukrainian soil
but I am certain that 20 years ago,
even 20 days ago,
in another valley so quiet
I could have heard my own breathing,
or along a lane sealed off from a city's bustle,
I would have seen another couple
kneeling, contentedly doing
the dirty work of readying a garden
for a summer surge
of tomatoes, peppers and cucumbers.

Now this couple and others may
still be kneeling, but no longer
are they to be found in their gardens,
where once lovingly tilled soil
is packed hard
with the print of tank treads,
and seeds planted
with seasonable optimism
are cheek by jowl
with shell casings
or mortar rounds
now cold as death,

all waiting
for their chance to explode.

~ Tom Gordon

Reconnections

PRIVATEERS

There are no greater allies
than the aged and the young.
I'm seventy, he's five, and
for now we're both alive
at the same time and what a time
it is we're having!
Son of my son, bright and brave,
from his deck
we skim the wave
of the wind-tossed Carib,
and we call our ship *The Raven*.

Merlin to his Arthur, I'm Chewbacca
to his Solo,
he for now my catechumen,
Robin Hoods upon the sea.
Plastic sabers clack, we sail
the back yard into glory
and gain a lasting treasure,
a subtle one to measure:
he creates, he intuits that what matters is the story.

The Raven is a fast ship,
not weighed down with heavy guns –
a Corsair trim and low,
made deliberate for boarding.
Sun and cookies, watermelon,
for training it's an ideal place

to learn what counts – love and valor, honor is
its own reward, and some things are
more important than the washing of your face.

Others are charged to guide his mind,
but I mean to shape his heart.
The young more recent come from God,
the elder on a reach for home,
from places on the edges can see
each other as a sign.

It's a natural alliance, the old man, the grandson.
I help him banish monsters;
perhaps someday he'll help with mine.

They despise us, call us Pirates,
but we favor "Privateers,"
fighting kings and mercantilers
from the shadow of the poor.
When hope pines for a sigil
but no sign of one is found,
lift your eyes to the horizon,
see the dark hull of *The Raven*,
standing off Barbados in the dawn.

~ SHANNON WEBSTER

On His First Day of Second Grade

I couldn't quite tell
if he was grinning.
His face covering seemed to
smile back at me.
A crooked, kaleidoscope caterpillar,
something he'd drawn before he could read or understand
the word, "pandemic."

Boundaries between my
feelings blurred,
of pride and anxiety,
exhaustion and confidence…
I'm not sure I ever knew
where one feeling started
and another began.

I've heard there's a thin line,
Between love and hate.
What's the line look like
between fear and sadness
or joy and revulsion?
Maybe, there's no line
at all.

Perhaps, like sputum
from this wretched illness,
fluid feelings mix to form
a mass, unrecognizable

in its contents, yet
unmistakable in its
vivid, scarlet coloring
and to hypo-camprian memories,
shocking in its
putrid smells

And still, I placed the car in it's
vein and waited to have him drawn
from my arms -- like each parental corpuscle that dutifully
trailed afterward – waiting in queue
to be blessed by the
white sanctifying
laser thermometer.
Light attesting to light.

And yet my flesh fears
That the blessed assurance
Of = or < 99.5 degrees presents
peace and love in cozy strokes
of monochrome arithmetical artifice,
knowing that lines of any weight
cannot in full faith
bear the whole
uncomfortable,
colorful
truth.

~ Mel Campbell

The Time Between Us

When we were young, how easy it was
to slip away and forget there was anyone
else in the world.

Our very being could fill time and
we could fold the hours
into a moment
securely hidden
in the small space between our hearts.
The dawn would arrive in midsentence
as we spoke of little things.

With the passing of the years
it became more difficult to imagine
the world – the one we alone inhabited,
the one supremely treasured,
the one where time was our own.
Unnumbered demands crowded
the space between our hearts
as the rhythms of life took hold.

We might forget that distant time,
were the memories not folded securely
and tucked away
like the hours we once held safely between us
until the first light of dawn.

~ Charles Kinnaird

Defiance

I can't balance budgets,
cure cancer,
hang above the rim.
At my age, I do not
snow-ski, water-ski, hang-glide,
install dishwaters,
conquer Kilimanjaro
wire my house,
mimic Monet
hit big-league pitching,
replicate the Wright Brothers,
walk on the moon,
become the next Bach,
wield sexual staying power.

But I can wave
at a neighbor,
compliment a stranger's attire.
lighten the load of the overburdened,
make pancakes for the home-bound,
go goofy with playful children,
offer hugs and not handshakes,
open my ears
to someone's words,
make eye contact with cashiers
and avoid a robot recital
of "Have a Nice Day."

Even as scoundrels
get their names on buildings and boulevards,
treat truth as a virus
and gleefully sow division,
I compliment a fellow shopper's striped dress,
openly admire that server's cool braids,
sing happy birthday to that woman
wearing the crown at an adjacent table,
every encounter a reason
to be happy, and defiant.

~ Tom Gordon

Been Painting My Boat

applying new varnish to sixty-five-year-old wood,
stained, yellowed in places, and sun blazed.
Time's worn well on my "Whirlwind,"
something I built
at the age of fourteen.
"You think you can do this
If I buy you the kit?"
"Oh, yes!" I replied.
"It's a man's project," Dad said,
"Meant to make you grow up."

I took on the challenge:
fifty pre-cut fir pieces,
two thousand brass screws,
a book of instructions,
a father's calculated dare.
two summer months
two months sweat and hard work.

I planed and sanded,
measured and drilled
Douglas fir plywood.
Boards screwed together--
fourteen feet long,
four feet in the beam,
the boat began to emerge—
a boy's wildest dream.

She's taken the waves

off Fripp Island in the Atlantic,
encountered turbulent passes,
at Gulf Shores, Destin, Mobile Bay.
Seafaring me with my parents,
and later my friends.
Then under my watchful eyes,
In storms or clear days,
my sons took the wheel,
each having his turn
at boat handling, fishing,
and safe navigation—
aboard this gift from my father,
I gave what I had been given.

~ Steve Coleman

Morning Light

Morning light comes through the window
reminding me of the softness
and splendor
of thought.

The light holds memories
flooding into the day:
of a six-year-old boy putting on
blue sneakers
soon to collect hillside dew;
of a happy mutt
sniffing along woodland trails;

As if early light
holds memories
breathed in over time,
stored for safe keeping –
first days of school,
blackberry picking,
first mornings on the job,
young love resting calmly
on the pillow –
memories to be awakened
as starlit nights fade
into the white gauze of dawn.

How silently the day comes forth
In this morning light
Where the heart can pause for a moment

before declaring any desire
or admitting any despair.

Making no demands,
this morning light lets me gather myself
before counting my losses.

~ Charles Kinnaird

Nice Ride

Fabulous, fluid L.A.,
Smoggy womb of car culture,
Cradle of the drive-in life:
Burgers and fries, movies and sighs,
Banks, dry-cleaners, churches—
Launder money, clothes, or souls
From the comfort of your front seat.

Hail the iconic hot-rodder,
The Eastside low-rider, the
Starlet cruising the Strip
With her top down.
Shiny and sexy, cars were costars
In Hollywood hits: cigarette-lit
Lovers parked for passion,
James Dean racing to the abyss,
Gangster getaways, Keystone Kops.

So many clowns, so many cars,
Think I in a freeway jam,
Preview of the apocalypse,
Life measured not in coffee spoons
But in miles per hour (or
Hours per mile). I inch to an exit
And take to the streets, the
Grand boulevards that unfurl
From downtown to the sea.
Palmy Sunset, pulsing Wilshire,

Mean-but-not-evil Pico,
And Santa Monica, last leg of
Route 66, ending at a pleasure pier,
Its Ferris wheel a neon mandala.

In L.A. the car was king,
Endless pavement its tribute.
"Nice ride," we wolf-whistled.
Today we sing the auto electric.
What will be lost when,
Instead of driving our cars,
They drive us?

~ Jeff Book

A Life at the Pool

The babies in diapers laugh and scream,
under the gaze of their parents,
with their toys and floaties,
unaware this is the best life will ever be.

Years later they're preening
at the lifeguard stand,
gaggling like magpies,
bathing in hormones and make up,
uniformed dress and tribal tattoos,
bored and impatient from waiting too long.

They return as beached whales,
basted with lotion,
with stretch marks and beer,
sunburns and novels,
recovering themselves
on their loungers and chairs.

Until they wobble and weave,
spectacles on noses,
bent over their canes,
on stork-thin legs,
watching the babies swim.

~ Roger Carlisle

Once and Then

Splintered pocked pier
weathered worn of disuse,
slime green lines
mooring waterlogged hulk.
Abandoned, unsailable,
half-sunken hull—
once spritely and strong
cutting a proud swath
sailing the seas.
Annual avid adventurers
Bahamas to Maine,
fifty-four-foot *Snowhawk*
sunny blue skies
dark stormy nights.

Petey, our captain,
wonderful provider of fun;
Dave, Stan, Randy, and Steve--
pleasure, adventure, escape.
Life-force ran along strong
on spray drenched deck;
in heeling high winds.
T'was top of the world,
and we were fine friends.
Then Pete died.
We grieved losing the great man,
who shared his good fortune
aboard *Snowhawk* at sea.

Half-beached, half-sunk now,
mainmast bent double,
white-hull greened,
one barnacled hulk.

I feel as she is,
Left only with memories,
Of fabulous days,
Surrendered to change,
 In the oceans of time.

~ Steve Coleman

Sights, Smells, Sounds

Stone Pathways

> "The stairs leading down to the water are cracked
> and marked by awakening"
> ~ Kazim Ali from "The Year of Summer"
> in *The Far Mosque*

At the basilica in Assisi
the sun highlighted a crack in one of the stone
    steps.
That crack awakened a joy reaching back
to my childhood.

A saint drew me to this Umbrian village
but it was a stone that reassured my steps – a
    stone
more ancient than words,
more constant than tradition.

The toddler knows the welcoming
of a stone along the path.
A schoolboy pockets that unusual rock
beckoning from beside the road
on his walk home.

The ancestors made stone circles,
Even moved quarried rock hundreds of miles
To the Salisbury Plain.
Countless others would stack a stone atop
    another
to mark a sacred encounter.

Pilgrims by the millions perform the Hajj each
    year
as they follow the Prophet.
Circling the clean-swept ground with
ancient prayers on their lips,
the focal point of their trek
is an ancient stone
marked by awakening.

Pebble pathways,
stone hearths
cornerstones in cityscapes –
human endeavors, all,
as we seek sure footing.

~ Charles Kinnaird

Photograph
Birmingham Bus Stop – 7 A.M.

I see her there as I drive past,
    Resting on a bench on a gritty city sidewalk,
        Awaiting the bus to the distant suburbs.

The thin, middle-aged, maple colored woman,
    Tilts slightly to her right, motionless,
        Hands folded neatly in her lap,

Her face inclined to catch, as if a kiss,
    The warm horizontal rays
        Of the early morning sun,

Frowning ever so slightly, worry lines gathered
    Round her tight mouth and shuttered eyes,
        Her eyelids glistening like gold.

One might assume she's merely basking in the sun,
    As immobile and placid as a meditating Buddha, or
        A young woman at the beach, book
        in her lap.

No, I think, more likely she's offering up a prayer,
    Gathering her strength, steeling herself to face
        The assured indignities of another day.

~ Chervis Isom

Piled Higher and Deeper

Succulents succeed
As others suck
Air from the room

Sickly sycophants
Cycle in circles
Circumvent synopses

Desiccants dry out
Diseases and mildew
Distribute dissertations

As scholars sidle
Slide alongside
Symphonies of silliness

Dust accumulates
On onion skin tomes
Lower shelves scream

Burdened by
Unread cultural histories
And literary lapses

Pantomimed as pearls
Wisdom scattered
Before swine trotters

Climate controlled
Storage sheds

Await

Sic transit gloria mundi.

~ Jim Ferguson

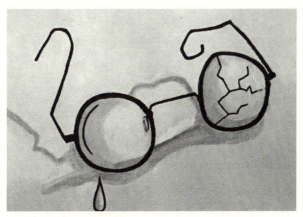

ILLUSTRATION BY VERONIQUE VANBLAERE

For Naught

(In memory of Phyllis Weinstein)

Through the display glass
I look upon remnants—
shoes of many sizes, mounds of suitcases,
spectacles to fit all sizes of faces.
Names of cities are inscribed on the luggage,
places where shoes, coats, hats and glasses were bought.

Once special possessions;
then all for naught.

As a little boy, it was a treat for me
to navigate the whirl of department stores

*and try on sneakers, trousers, shirts and what's more,
eat lunch in a place where I would sit up straight
and get some ice cream when I cleaned my plate.*

Were my merry-go moments the same for those

whose piles of possessions have come to rest here?
Who doesn't want to live and shop without fear?
But death, with no discount, was all they could buy
 'neath the mocking sign of Arbeit Macht Frei.

~ Tom Gordon

Philosophy 101

It starts with epistemology –
how do you know you know what you know?
The solipsist makes no apology,
asserting the self alone is quantum,
and Immanuel Kant but Genghis Kahn
and therein lies a problem.

Cogito ergo Descartes est.
Words and hours have been squandered
on whether reality exists,
but if we wait around a bit,
conspiracy theorists will show up.
They really love solipsist shit!

Rational, material, ideal,
metaphysical, and do we care
so long as the thing itself is real?
Per another great philosopher,
  "It's still not weird enough for me."*
So take another offer.

It is worth spending more time here,
if the world is less idea than place.
So sit down there, pull up a chair,
and let me tell you where it starts –
This tavern, *this* beer, *that* young cowboy
on stage singing out his heart.

~ Shannon Webster

*Hunter Thompson

Cleaving

Fossil-fuel fires
cleave icebergs
glaciers weep to the sea
cellphones vibrate the airways
bees die
plastic waste surges oceans
polar caps melt
thunderstorms rage
Earth suffers its
Ending Age
Society cleaves apart
fears fire hatred
confound logic
Babel's tower crumbles
under tons of lies.
Ethos sinks into the abyss
misspoken, mendacious babble
chanted to tribal drums
while hate grows great
Legacy for our lost children

~ Steve Coleman

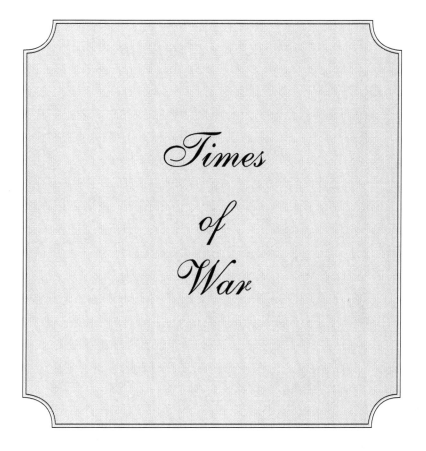

Times of War

Resignation
(March 2022)

We are in a time
where we can attend
exhibitions of awful things
without leaving our living rooms.

So it is
with the latest war's raw material
of anguish, devastation,
protest and truth-mocking
justification.

Meanwhile, painters, poets,
musicians, filmmakers and photographers
are sorting through images and thoughts,
adding to their files,
preparing for the day
when their work will fill
museum walls, concert halls,
pages of anthologies,
aid organization leaflets and web pages,
and big screens at multiplexes.

People will attend exhibitions and screenings,
line up at book signings,
buy the CD, make donations.
I will be among them.
But don't expect me to close my eyes,

shake my head,
put my hand to my mouth,
or let the spillways
below my eyes
feel the flow of tears.
I am old and numb now,
all too aware
of the empty power
of the words, "Never Again."

~ Tom Gordon

The Blood of Patriots

Strife-tossed refugees in a *Times* photo,
Uprooted, perhaps twigs from my family tree,
Mother and daughters bearing the maiden name
Of my mother, whose parents left Ukraine for
The steppes of Canada, blessedly before
The pogroms, the Eastern Front, Stalin's famine.
She played the piano well, even Liszt's
Barn-storming etudes, like the one
Inspired by Mazepa, the Ukrainian officer
Who rallied troops against the Tsar's army.

But my Ukrainian heritage is thin, apart from
Plump pierogies my mother and aunts made.
Now like so many I feel a keen kinship with
My Slavic brethren, defending lines drawn in
Rich black earth against a seismic onslaught.
Proxies for arm's-length allies, their raw
Patriotism makes us question our own courage.
What would we do if dystopia became destiny?
A self-styled Tsar seeks to feast on their blood.
Who can drive a stake through his heart?

~ Jeff Book

You, Vladimir

So people are praying as they have before,
but the sky still reigns with pitiless shells.
God stands impotent as you wage your war
while the damned raise toasts in the depths of hell.
Cities, families destroyed for a lie,
Whatever is done, you say it's their fault.
Indifferent to truth, you won't hear the cry
of mothers whose children repose in vaults.
I see your face and I wish upon you
a suffering death you cannot foresee.
Its grip so tight, your coward's face so blue,
But my hate for you is poisoning me.
So I cry as Ukraine reels from this strife:
Why do you hold such a firm lease on life?

~ Tom Gordon

What Can We Do?

Ganglion convoys--
awkward, armored tank tenacles
slither through cities
blast buildings, crush towns,
smother hopes in smoldering ash,
sadistic destruction of people
who want to be free.
What can we do?

Pull together as NATO
But do not provoke Putin?
Fingers ready to trigger
nuclear-nothingness.
Cynical tsaristic war
Wrought by solipsistic Ivan;
no one dare say,
Vladimir, my dear,
You're severely crazy?

Our allied violence
Threatens only the world.
Knowing we're fighting
A brain-twisted snake,
What shall we make?
A nuclear first-strike?
Surely no one wins,
Everyone dies.

Who then can defeat him?

Sanctions will bleed him,
Russians can wage internal revolt;
Blinded by czars, Stalin's USSR,
Historical losses are all they know.

How can we aid Ukraine
When our own nation
Is hobbled by
Internal squabble?
Tune media to your own
Selection of liars;
In our own great nation
Tunnel vision
Trounces truth.
While pernicious Putin plods on.

Will the final event
Be etched in atomically radiant stone?
We hoped for better
But an insane oligarch could ruin all
And do it all alone?
~ Steve Coleman

Bricks in Kyivian Gates

Walking the streets to the
Golden Gate, feeling footfalls on rubble,
As the ruble falls, hope dims dingy in smoke and blast.
You can marvel as sirens wail at this enshrined imposter
Less monument to medieval glories than
An intentional reminder of a red, menacing millstone.

Yet, what do its bricks think of war?

They are not ancient, worn before Solzhenitsyn, Shevchenko
or Shakespeare.
The sand, clay, lime and iron, elementally,
Do not yield.
Blow them up.
Use them to build a fortress against tanks and tyranny.
The notes that form the binding chords remain.

But the music of those bricks…
Like a Picture at an Exhibition (and its Kyiv Gate) --
Triumphant, immoveable, and overwhelming notes,
They march, pitch by pitch,
Brave bogatyrs, each of them, to transcendent heights,
Resting on regal thirds and lush chords, together,
Moving unstoppingly,
Bound in this piece by the mortar of bars and staffs.

In time immemorial, the noble and the knave
Strike cymbalic blows, drum up support,
Blow house and life apart …

For freedom and ancient grievances
Or a nice piece of beach-front property.
While the bricks simply remain where they lay,
Equally collecting blood of babies, knights and cowards.

~ Mel Campbell

AFTER THE WAR

"The time will come when we will be able to sleep,
but it will be after the war, after the victory."
– Ukraine President Voldymyr Zelenskyy

When things get quiet again,
we will take a walk.
We'll find a street
like that one off Weldon's Circle,
with the coffee shop
next to the record store
where we first heard *Tuxedo Junction*
sung by The Manhattan Transfer.
Surely, there will be a street
like that one again.

We will remember a time
when the pieces fit –
when we could imagine
building a home of our own.

I took those years for granted
until they stretched into a decade
of dull routine –
the everyday greyness
of riding to work,
shopping for groceries,
watching the Nightly News.

We could numb ourselves

to rumors of war
until the missile strikes lit the night.
Crumbled concrete cascaded
from buildings to sidewalk
and into the streets
Roadways crowded
with newly awakened refugees –
homebodies turned migrants.

Twisted bridges
bombed out buildings
neighborhoods in rubble –
we had seen it before on the Nightly News,
always in some distant land
until the war machine shattered our lives

Baldwin Street! That was it –
The one off Weldon's Circle.
The one with the record store.
We'll find it again
after the war.

~ Charles Kinnaird

This Is Not Ukraine

Snow beckons from the Alps,
but the spring sun holds court,
as do calls of the unhurried,
the greasy fragrance
from sizzling wurst,
the sleep-inducing trill
of an onrushing stream.

Those understudied
by days of routine
find stages today.
Blackbirds with orange beaks
and orange eye rings
sing like auditionists.
Two ducks who live in a wooden house
find a stream's eddy
and rub against each other.
Laughter drifts through trees
from a beer garden;
the fastest moving things
are honeybees
buzzing bouquets of blue flowers
and children running
and pumping the pedals of bikes.
An old, bald mustachioed man
walks his Dachshund,
a blonde blue-eyed girl
holding hands with her Oma

smiles at me,
a kerchiefed Muslim mother
guides her son
to a harness on a zip line.

A day's drive away,
a country is at war.
People from there are here,
and in a corner bereft of laughter,
where her beer has gone tepid
and her sandwich is damp,
a woman tells new friends
of bird-shaped buns, boiled dumplings and
sunflower fields back home,
where a shell hole is all that remains
of her father.

~ Tom Gordon

APPOMATTOX

I feel both weariness and relief
at the mere mention of this place –
the desperate struggles,
the losses,
the ruinous battles
when the air was filled with smoke
and my stomach tight
with only yesterday's hardtack
to fuel my body.

There is a dream if I can find it –
maybe I saw it scattered on the ground –
but my, how dreams evaporate
when brother fights brother.
Caught between the will to go on
and the urge to turn back,
I want nothing more than to hear
frogs along the creek bank
and crickets in the field
the way they sang my day
to an end
as I sat on the back steps.

At Appomattox
the fighting stops.
My body is glad for the reprieve
but my mind races on –
where is that dream,

The one we held to?
Generations pass.
Frogs along the creek bank
and crickets at night
mend my soul over time
until I can find the dream –
the one that moved us all
to lay down our arms,
to build houses on tree lined streets,
to buy a snow cone at the ballpark.

Then comes the dissonant trumpet sound
from over the hill.
Frantic cries that the enemy is at the gate,
accusations left and right,
brother fights against brother,
households divided,
anger over Critical Race Theory,
hostility to vaccinations.

I walk out to the back steps,
listen for crickets,
and long for Appomattox.

~ Charles Kinnaird

Good Love/ Bad Love

The Day Before Easter: A Prose Poem

We were children then, about six years old or thereabouts, playing on the grassy lawn in front of the apartment building which sat across the street from the little house in which I grew up, so long ago I've forgotten the names of my friends, forgotten their faces, forgotten the games we played, but I've remembered these long years, seventy of them, that specific Saturday morning, the day before Easter, when it happened, a spring day as sunny and bright as one would hope for an Easter weekend -- a time of re-awakening after winter, a time of re-birth, of coming to life -- and I still remember his face, the father of my little friend, as he emerged from his car holding something in his hands, a huge smile on his face as he came into our play group extending his hands for his son to see his Easter gift, and we gathered around to see as well, and what we saw was a sight I'll never forget, a frightened little duckling huddling in his hands, which should have been yellow but for Easter had been dyed an unnatural unthinkable pink, and a wave of sorrow washed over me for that little bundle of fear,

for I too felt as helpless and alone in that
instant as it must have felt, its feathers a
hideous pink, embarrassed as if It were naked,
and no mother anywhere in sight for him to
hide under the cover of her wing.

After showing us the duckling, he put it on
the sidewalk, pride on his face, as the
duckling began to stretch there in the shadow
of all those larger hulking bodies, to take a
tentative step, and we boys were gathered too
closely I suppose, because his son made a false
step and suddenly the little duckling was partly
beneath his foot, at which a shadow passed
over his father's face as he batted the boy away,
cursing him for his clumsiness, and we all
watched for a moment as the duckling
fluttered but could not stand. Then the man
snatched up the duckling, examined it for only a
moment, and saw its leg was crushed. His face
turned scarlet with rage as he began to curse
the boy, and in one teeth-clenching, struggling
jerk, he wrenched the duckling's head from its
body and threw the parts on the sidewalk
before us, quivering pink feathers blotted in blood.

We looked on in horror, then scattered like
quail on the rise, each his own way, and we
did not return, not that day nor for many days
afterwards. I've always wondered about that

little boy, who burst into tears as it happened. He had nowhere to run, to hide, like the rest of us. And the man? How does a man leap from kindness to cruelty in the blink of an eye? And did he too, like us, remember for all the days of his life what he had done? And did each of us boys, in turn and in his own time, unlearn the lesson that father taught us about what it means to be a man?

~ Chervis Isom

Rembrandt's Prodigal Son
(Hermitage Museum, St. Petersburg, Russia)

The father dominates the frame
with his warm forgiving smile,
hands crossed without martyrdom,
bending over to embrace the lost son, oblivious
to the jealous frown of the elder son,
whose entitlement has destroyed civilizations
for centuries.

~ Roger Carlisle

Steel City Eurydice

A foot – stirrupped underneath –
gently rocks her silver wheelchair,
rebellious, out of step with
a steeled city where
the dead live, and
the living die daily.
So, she dances and smiles –
confined to a tarnished throne –
as shades and shadows pass
aware and unattentive.

Once, she may have
straightened her then-blonde
locks primping for a lover –
her movements constrained only by a
hillbilly father or the Savior she feared.
Now her mind clangs on boney prison bars,
as slowly, imperceptivity, palsy stiffens
her cells and ushers her
toward darkness.

But today, defiant, she
raises hands, stretches,
and breathes in her freedom,
embracing her protector, love-locked with her.
And as he does each day,
he removes comb and brush
from her dirtied pack and singing quietly,

works her army of silvery, long hairs –
bent, tired and entangled
from a night's work as bastion
from cardboard and plastic bag pillows.

Together, they hold court,
under shade of crepe myrtle and magnolia,
and if asked, he will cross
the asphalt river or play his music and harp
to fetch crumb coins floating
from fattened fingers…
for her.

And as he turns to receive
their daily dross, as he did
yesterday, and yesterdays,
bartering for their souls,
she touches his weathered arm,
and squeezes it with
fingers, hardening,
as they hope
and part.

And returning his gaze toward her,
he offers thanks, not for
conditional charity, but
that her foot rocks one more time,
and her light, though
flickering,
remains.

~ Mel Campbell

Omelets and Petals

I see it still,
that first Sunday morning.
On the phone,
you said you were making omelets.
Minutes later, I watched you do it,
not saying much,
feeling warmth from your kitchen,
letting my thoughts waft
toward what might come later.

Later came.
So did other Sundays with omelets
when I no longer watched
but sliced onions and peppers
and set the table
as you wielded the spatula,
eyed the floppy yellow disc
bubbling in the skillet,
then tilted your face to allow
my advancing lips to brush
your cheek.

That cheek.
I have not kissed it in years.
But I will always see it
as a delicacy, a privilege,
as pink with promise
as the fresh rose petals

in bloom outside.

Those blooms fade,
the petals fall,
but when I tuck them in my palm,
I recall the comforting sizzle
from a pan upon a stove,
my lips warm and eager
for a next move
not mine to take,
but yours to approve.

~ Tom Gordon

Northwest Passage

I cannot claim to have found it
Ghost coast in whale bone laced
Misted whistled rocketed shore
Current-carved wave-racked line
Boulder-buoyed jagged coast
Purple majesty-jutted sky
Unreachable untouchable peaks
Conifer-valleyed nestled ladened
Bear and beavered salmon-filled rivers
Gold flowing glittered and geyser fed
Steaminess shrouded rock sheltered
Vaulted and vast vacuous land, yet
I
Searched dreaming of not-known
Cast glaciered glances
Graceless unseeing
Eye
Fathomed a path mythologized foam
Sailed iceberg bays and midnight days
Frigid nothingness frosted air
Arrived not here but there
And in my unknowing discovered
You.

~ Jim Ferguson

A Cruel Rain

The sun was crowded by
a rain-dark cloud.
Juniper and sage, rabbit-brush,
thrust up thirsty branches,
thinking to break their fast.
Rain fell in a gray sheet,
visible for fifty miles as
long lines descending
in the dry air and arid heat.
It vanished, vaporized. Virga
that never touched earth,
it offered only hope
and proffered only dust.

Like that one day in El Paso
where I stood on the assigned corner,
my head filled with her,
my heart filled with her.
Feeling ever more worry
as time passed, I held my post.
I waited long, 137 minutes,
before I left.

~ Shannon Webster

Slip Knot

My marriage was a silken bond,
Like the four-in-hand I tied on our
Wedding day, a knot that, cinched tight,
Is hard to undo, like a hangman's noose.

Our differences were foxhole synergy,
Complementary, or so I believed.
How they became something else,
Sand in the gears, fueling friction—
The wrong kind of heat—is hard to fathom.

We had potent chemistry, traveled widely.
We paddled as one, buoyant as a
Whitewater raft, or so I believed.
In the plague years we grew a bit apart
Then back together, like twining vines,
Or so I believed.

But somehow we came untied.
Affection ebbed slowly, despite efforts
To revive it, life became too routine.
The keen savor we'd shared faded,
As if we'd traded steak for tofu,
Gay Paree for the farm.

Don't share another of your poems
Unless it's about me, she said,
Only half joking. The ode I started
To her warm heart and womanly allure,

Her playful wit and clever ways,
Remains unfinished.

Our bond was strong enough to
Belay any reach, summit any peak,
Or so I believed. But it proved to be
A slip knot, undone with a yank, like
Popping a parachute.

Except a slip knot is a hitch in one rope
And we are now two, unhitched, frayed.
The twining vines severed,
The raft foundering, adrift.
After the rapids the bailing begins.

~ Jeff Book

The Anomaly: A Sonnet

It's in the nature of things that we age;
Time bears humanity in its slipstream,
And we heedlessly draft, as in a dream;
Birthdays stops us cold; we turn back the page.

We look at photos from our youth and gauge
The years that have elapsed along the beam
Of time and flinch at images we deem
So . . . obsolete. Do we despair . . . or do we rage?

Will we accept who we've become with grace?
As you, my love, have done, with equanimity,
Your faith suppressing incipient fear.

Delicate laugh lines etch your pretty face,
My love, yet you're the anomaly;
More beautiful you are each passing year.

~ Chervis Isom

Final Course

For Bill Buckner

A hero won the 1980 batting title.
An All-Star, a contact hitter wearing
High-top black cleats many an unceremonious
Day, defying his aching ankles.

Yet in every replay, the small, cowhide ball
Still dribbles underneath the glove
Of someone I was rooting for,
An error and something like that.

As many times as I've watched it,
As many times as I've hoped that
The outcome would change,
It never has.

I'd made the same mistake a thousand times
Letting the ball sneak through,
And no Bambino curse or death threats followed,
Just mortification for myself.

And I would put myself back out
On the field and try not to make
The same mistake again …
To only, eventually, scream to heaven.

He couldn't silence the brokenhearted boos
Any more than I could control
Where or how the tricky hops went or
How old bones creak and grow more disagreeable.

A man may miss a grounder

And die a thousand deaths,
But my Buckner trots out
The next inning ... and innings
Until fields yield to pastures,
Similarly ambivalent and green,
Still leaving labored, fading impressions,
Because that is where a man
Chose to leave his cleat marks.

~ Mel Campbell

Scene from My Father's Wake

Clean shaven, well-groomed mustache,
debonair in death
when in his later years
he had been too tired to shave
and often did not bother
to find a clean shirt –
the rumpled one sufficed.
Once, I had offered to help him shave
but he put me off
with the wave of the hand.

My Pop,
now in a dark suit,
is laid out for viewing
in the small-town church.
The circle is tightly gathered
as family and friends
speak softly.
There is a moment of calm
in a time of grief.

My daughter
pulls a white flower
from one of many funeral wreaths
in the room.
She asks me to lift her up
so she can look down into
my father's casket

where she carefully tucks
that single blossom
into his breast pocket.

~ Charles Kinnaird

Those Emerald Green Eyes: A Villanelle

In her bed, unmoving, my mother lies
And follows me with her emerald green eyes.

In her bed, unmoving, my mother pries.
"When have you seen your daddy?" Her plain fears
Paralyze my heart; I contemplate lies.

She drills me with her furious, green eyes.
Shall I tell the truth? I can't bear her tears.
In her bed, unmoving, my mother tries

Once more to move me with her keen, green eyes.
Shall I falsify? Pacify her fears?
Those suspicious green eyes loom far too wise.

She'd never believe some half-hatched device;
Yet the truth may trigger a surge of tears.
I clench my lips, avert my guilty eyes.

In her bed, unmoving, my mother sighs,
"I think your daddy's just quit me." She peers,
Her bewildered green eyes immobilize

My desperate attempt to temporize.
"Daddy died six months ago." My heart sears.
Those startled, green eyes spring wide in surprise.
My God! A hundred times my father dies.

~ Chervis Isom

A Family Listens to Their Mother

We strain to hear our mother's failing voice
as cancer consumes her life;
we stand in the hall of her old house listening.
Every morning, talking to herself, she says--
"get up, try harder, don't quit."

She tries to rise on stork-thin legs,
her face confused, wasting into shadow.

We see our warrior fading,
her voice falls down and down,
we hold her upright,
wishing she could fly.

~ Roger Carlisle

NEXT

Post-op dark and strange,
octopal I-V, Oximeter, EKG;
manacled agony,
monitor-shrouded bed--
uncertain future,
no relief expected.

Hurts to move,
frightens to lie still.
"So, what is your pain?"
rush-by nurse asks uncaring.
"Do you rate another pill?"

Then a Patient Care Tech,
a savior arrives--
a true mammoth,
pot-bellied black man.

"I'll give you a bath,"
"Pull you out of bed."
Strips and washes,
rough but gentle,
gushing soggy swash.

Aware in hospital dimness
a ham hand tugs me up--
thunder-rolling,
wave-breaking pain.

I stand on my feet
to wrestle the giant,
lay my hand on his shoulder
to steady my weakened frame.

He has me hang on.
"Walk down the hall,"
Which looks ever long.
"No worry, I got you, my man."

I am up walking,
free from Tantalus' rock,
hurting, but human,
shocking return to myself.

Out of self-focused fog,
my savior inhales hard;
this big man who helps me
has issues himself.

"Hear your own breathing?"
I ask, holding on.
"Yeah, I'm gonna start running again,"
he pants, struggling along.
Melding our suffering--mine and his--
performing our morbid dance
down the in-hospitable hall,
we each silently wonder
who first will be called.

~ Steve Coleman

Extremities

In the Civil War, sepsis would
Finish grape shot's grim job.
Military doctors amputated
Shattered limbs with dispatch.
Whiskey and leather, vised
In pain-clamped jaws, served
Where opioids were, unlike
Our time, in short supply.
Outside field hospitals,
Phantomized limbs would
Mount in desperate piles
Cast away, carted away,
Spent chips in war's
Casino of carnage.

During the fourth and final
Operation on my arm,
I revive to witness the
Rebellious appendage
Numbed and tourniqueted,
Parted like the Red Sea.
As directed, I flex the tendon
Freed of scar tissue, shining
White in the pitiless light.
Now, with its serial scars,
I call it my Frankenstein arm.
My therapist uses electrodes
To zap it, firing the muscle.

Cue the villagers with pitchforks,
I say. She laughs, as the current
Mounts and my hand twitches
In a sad simulacrum of normal.
My once-deft typing is now that
Of an old whiskey-in-the-drawer
Newsman, hunting and pecking,
Snatching the ink-black phone:
Sweetheart, get me Rewrite!
But no, this is the last draft.
I've donated my old clarinet.

~ JEFF BOOK

Letting Go

It is the season of relinquishment,
    of stopping, letting go.

The baton is lowered;
    the last instrument case closes.
Ledgers return to folios,
    monitors go dark.
Lesson plans are filed away,
    lunch boxes close for the last time.
No lab report prints out,
    nor law demands redress.
No Bible opens, no saw reciprocates;
    it is the season of relinquishment.

The alarm does not rouse the sleeper,
    the calendar lists no rite to attend.
No vessel languishes at dock, waiting;
    rails and runways lie bare,
Lifts and limos afford no transport;
    there is nowhere to be.
The page lies vacant;
    obligation is in retreat.
No rule but liberty maintains,
    and lasting room for wonder.

It is the time of letting go;
    the season of relinquishment.

~ Shannon Webster

The Human Spirit

We are born into exile, each Man thrust
Into a vale of tears where he must learn
This Proverb, "Remember, Man, you are dust
And unto dust you shall return."

From ancient times the perpetual,
The existential Question has rung,
Why are we here, and for what eventual
Destination, what Purpose, have we sprung?

Why are our days not haunted by the dread
Recognition of *memento mori*,
The remembrance we all shall soon be dead,
Our lives no more than a meaningless story?

Yet Mankind is infused with a spirit,
An inexhaustible flame of divinity,
Yearning to build beyond our limit,
For the benefit of posterity.

That spirit fired ancient generations to build
Towering Cathedrals high above the field,
That same spirit now endows the human will
To soar into the heavens on wings of steel.

~ Chervis Isom

Frozen Ground

I remember the winter when my mother left.
My dad and I walked bare frozen
ground on the Nebraska farm, no trees,
just a few broken stalks of corn.
 "Your mom is gone," he said.
"Don't worry, everything will be OK."

I was nine.

We were visiting my grandparents' farm.
I kept asking where my mother had gone,
listening to family whisperings, receiving
no answers, stunned
by how quickly people disappear.

Years later, I learned from my father
the unspeakable truth:
She had been in a mental hospital,
too crazy to be mentioned,
too ill to be seen.

Now, I still live in that frozen moment
in the corn field, walking with my Dad.
I never ask for help,
expect no one to listen.

~ Roger Carlisle

Palm Sunday

Calm Palm Sunday morning
The tornado passed over
Calm Palm Sunday now

Calm, calm Palm Sunday morning
Holy Week begun with all its
Harm and resurgence

Balm, balm, Palm Sunday morning
Fronds uncurl, twirl, betray no
Qualm, blades unsheathed slashing

Alms, alms, lay down palms
Pollen bombs with yellow
Napalm, bombs, bombs yet

Psalm, psalm, memory of psalms
Maundy Thursday sure to follow
Calm, calm, Palm Sunday morning.

~ Jim Ferguson

The End

Because we can no longer see
Because the stars no longer shine
We think this is the end of things—
Bright fancy shiny lovely things—
Fallen like the autumn leaves
From faded trees, and brown
Decay's scent left to linger on
And on and on and ever on

But no; a turning of the path
The liquid bending of the stone
The gentle rising of the tide
The confidence of God alone
Speaks, and more certain than
The garbled hissing of the end.

~ Jim Ferguson

What Remains

Watching from a Distance

Pee Wee buried Phin in the flower bed,
where the soil felt softer, and the memories
silently cycled like amber leaves of last year.
The woman had slowed, tried to avoid him,
but the excited puppy burst from the yard,
matching pliable body to vulcanized rubber.
My adult daughter watched it happen, heard
the whimpers, and the pup's blood stained
her Old Navy sweater and dried
to her cheeks and blond hair,
as she clung last pangs against her mothering chest.

She'd come with the pup –
the one she and her husband picked together,
right before he shipped out.
She'd come to help Granny and Pappy –
to hang the familiar Christmas decorations,
wrap presents and purge the
out-of-date pantry excesses.
Now, she held hands with family,
white-haired and slouching
toward eternity.

The grandparent feet no longer could
safely push spade into soil
to offer the pitiful bundle final resting.
So, Mom called Pee Wee,
who'd, two-weeks before, collected

my father from the floor
as he struggled to stand, piss or hold his dignity.

She left her pup's belongings behind,
loaded her car, and drove
to the birthday party 100 miles away,
number 12, for her sister –
a party she'd not expected to be able to attend
on a day now marked by
permanent images of impermanence.

"Maybe this is a sign; I'm about to be 30, you know," she
said, standing in my kitchen
and inches taller than me,
and now only in shadow the little girl that needed
crinkly leaves dusted from her head.

"I don't know what I should do, Dad," she quivered,
"But I think I want to take a shower."

~ Mel Campbell

INCREDO

I do not believe in Believing.
What you mean is, "I think," or "It is my opinion."
I don't believe in belief as a pass into heaven
nor that God metes out reward and punishment,
nor that I will someday walk hand-in-paw with Jesus,
nor that virtue very often pays its own way,
nor that guys in the white hats always win.

But I do believe in the worth of the poet's potion–
love, beauty and a 20-year old single malt.

I do not believe
help drawn from self-help paperbacks,
I do not think it likely
the USA is the world's best nation,
I do not believe
I will be long remembered after I'm gone,
I do not find veracity in
politicians, preachers, or economists.
I am not persuaded
there is such a thing as progress;

And yet… belief aside…I am amazed…
by morning light glowing through dewdrop on a leaf,
at the deft, alluring voice of Segovia's guitar,
and the way she looks in sleep as I bring
her first cup of coffee.

~ Shannon Webster

Oblation

Wake slowly into stillness
so silent ears ring seeking referent.

This day no engine startles from the road below,
no snarling chain saw rattles the canyon walls.

This day no stalking wind finds the pines;
Piñon and Ponderosa stand silent sentinels.

The dogs lie dumb and dormant.

The elastic cat stretches and recoils
ever so slow back into position.

A dove calls a single comment and falls mute.

There come those rare and gentle days of
tranquility and calm. Soon the Woman will stir,

and soft from the kitchen will come muffled
sound, the clink of a spoon on a mug's edge.

We will share unhurried the coffee sacrament,
and rise into a holy Saturday blessed by
dearth of demand, absence of obligation.

There come those consecrated days of the
purity of being, the grace of simplicity.

Be still, and know…

~ Shannon Webster

Contributor Biographies

Jeff Book, over a long career as a writer and editor, has covered travel, food, design, and other topics on six continents. His work has appeared in *Departures, GQ, Smithsonian, Travel & Leisure, Coastal Living, The Los Angeles Times, Elle Décor*, and other publications. In pursuit of stories, he has schmoozed with famous subjects, snorkeled with sea lions in the Sea of Cortez, sailed on dry land in the Mojave Desert, and jumped out of a perfectly good airplane over Alabama. His furniture designs have been shown in California galleries. He is grateful that poems don't also have to serve as seating.

Mel Campbell is a husband, father, racquetball enthusiast, part-time coach and blogger, and frequent remover of spiders, insects and other creepy crawly invaders from his Birmingham, Alabama, Highland Avenue home. He has worked for some 30 years as a professional writer, editor and communicator, providing counsel on messaging, planning, crisis communication, public relations and storytelling, He is a graduate of the University of Montevallo and holds a master's degree in English from the University of Alabama.

Roger Carlisle is a 77-year-old semi-retired physician, married with two children. He currently lives in Birmingham and works in a free medical clinic for the poor. He grew up in Oklahoma and was a history major in college. He has been writing poetry for ten years and has published 44 poems in various magazines and poetry journals.

Steve Coleman is a graduate of Indian Springs School, earned a Bachelor of Arts in history from Duke University and a Master of Arts in

English from University of Alabama. He is married to the former Dr. Sumter M. Carmichael, a psychiatrist. Steve has been a naval officer, a high school teacher, a businessman, and commercial real estate broker. After retiring in 2009, he now enjoys sailing, writing and landscape painting. He has authored biographies and histories of local interest, magazine articles, novels and poetry. His story, "The Meanest Man in Pickens County," was the first place (state) winner in the 2013 Hackney Literary Awards for short stories. He has published three novels: *The Navigator: A Perilous Passage, Evasion at Sea* and *The Navigator II: Irish Revenge. André's Reboot: Striving to Save Humanity* has won Honorable Mention from *Writer's Digest*; a Silver Medal from Independent Publisher Book Awards 2020; and was awarded Distinguished Favorite by NYC Big Book Award 2021. See his website: stephenbcoleman.com

Jim Ferguson Residing in the Birmingham, Alabama area, James (Jim) Ferguson writes poems and prose by night, and practices life and law by day. He remembers living in a pre-digital world and is wondering what a post-second-Elizabethan era will bring. His work is rarely offered for publication and seldom if ever awarded prizes. He is thankful for having been published by the *Birmingham Arts Journal, The Almost Dead Poets Society,* and his high school literary journal *Spectrum*.

Tom Gordon, a native of Houston, Texas, has spent most of his adult life in Alabama, working as an editor and reporter at *The Anniston Star*, and as a reporter and part-time editor at *The Birmingham News*. He has contributed articles and photographs to *B Metro Magazine*, as well as photographs and poems to the Highland Poets' first publication, "The Social Distance," a volume of pandemic poetry published in 2020. He has poems published in *Birmingham Arts Journal* and *Aura Literary Arts Review,* and partnered with Birmingham artist Veronique Vanblaere on "An Artist and a Poet Walk into a Coffee Shop," a 2021 exhibition of haikus and paintings. Gordon holds a bachelor's degree in political science from the University of Alabama, where he was the lead plaintiff in a 1970 lawsuit challenging the university's decision to ban Yippie leader Abbie Hoffman from speaking on campus. Tom also has a master's degree in journalism from the University of Missouri and spent the year 1981 reporting and writing in Europe and West Africa.

Chervis Isom grew up in Birmingham and attended Birmingham public schools. He earned a BA degree from Birmingham-Southern College [1962] and a J.D. from Cumberland School of Law [1967]. He practiced law with Berkowitz, Lefkovits, Isom & Kushner, which merged into Baker Donelson Bearman Caldwell & Berkowitz in 2003, and continued with the merged firm until his retirement in 2021. Chervis published a memoir in 2014, *The Newspaper Boy: Coming of Age in Birmingham, Alabama During the Civil Rights Era*. The book earned a Starred Review from Kirkus, which named the memoir among the Best Books of 2015. Chervis is presently engaged in the writing of a novel and another memoir, and he says there's nothing he likes better than pushing words around. See thenewspaperboy.net.

Charles Kinnaird is a writer whose career choices have included teaching, social work, and healthcare. A native of Alabama, he has also lived and worked in Hong Kong, and California. He has maintained a love for writing sharing some of his poetry and essays on his blog, *Not Dark Yet* at https://notdarkyet-commentary.blogspot.com. His work has been published in the *Birmingham Arts Journal*, and *Avant Appalachia*. Charles resides in Birmingham, Alabama with his wife, Vicki, where they enjoy gardening and birdwatching.

J. Shannon Webster grew up in New Mexico's 4 Corners area playing songs for short cash. Musician, community organizer, pastor and lecturer, he is recipient of the NAACP AL's Community Service Award, recognized by President Obama for his social justice work in Birmingham. Author of too many papers, articles, and manuals, he has released three independent albums of his songs, the most recent recorded in Muscle Shoals.

Made in the USA
Middletown, DE
11 October 2023